DOGS HELPING PEOPLE

Police Dogs

Helping to Fight Crime

Alice B. McGinty

The Rosen Publishing Group's
PowerKids Press™
New York

Published in 1999 by The Rosen Publishing Group, Inc.
29 East 21st Street, New York, NY 10010

First Edition

Book Design: Michael de Guzman

Photo Credits and Illustrations: p. 4 © Larry Grant/FPG International; p. 7 © Robert Maier/Animals Animals; p. 8 © Charlie Palek/Animals Animals; pp.11, 19, 20 by Kelly Hahn; p. 12 © Norvia Behling/Animals Animals; p. 15 © Ron Chapple/FPG International; p. 16 © J. Pickerell.

McGinty, Alice B. (Alice Blumenthal)
    Police dogs: helping to fight crime / by Alice B. McGinty.
        p.   cm. — (Dogs helping people)
    Includes index.
    Summary: Explores the selection, training, and uses of police dogs in fighting crime.
    ISBN 0-8239-5218-5
    1. Police dogs—Juvenile literature. [1. Police dogs 2. Dogs.]
    I. Title. II. Series.
HV8025.M34 1998
363.32'32—dc21
                                          97-52013
                                           CIP
                                         AC

Manufactured in the United States of America

Contents

German shepherds are often chosen to be police dogs because they are smart and strong.

Jesse's Busy Nose

Jesse is a **German shepherd** (JER-mun SHEH-perd) puppy with a busy nose. Jesse sniffs the ground. Jesse sniffs the air. Jesse knows his family and his toys by the way they smell.

Andy Charles is a police officer. He wants a special partner to help him on **patrol** (puh-TROHL). He talks with the police department. He talks with his family. Everyone agrees that Officer Charles should have a special partner. He decides to get a police dog. Officer Charles likes Jesse's busy nose. He wants Jesse to be his new partner.

Police Dogs

    Dogs have protected people and property for hundreds of years. The first training school for police dogs opened in Germany around 1920. Today, dogs are an important part of police squads in many countries.

    Why do the police use dogs? Dogs can do some things better than people can. Dogs can smell things that people can't smell. Dogs hear things that people can't. Dogs can also run faster than people. Police dogs are trained carefully to use their skills to help police officers fight crime.

A dog's sense of smell and sense of hearing are very strong. They are ▷ even stronger than a human's.

6

K-9 Training School

   Officers and their dogs are trained at **K-9**, or **canine**, (KAY-nyn) Training Schools. K-9s are another name for police dogs. The officers have chosen their K-9 partners carefully. The dogs are healthy, well-mannered, and between one and two years old.

   Like many police dogs, these K-9s are male German shepherds. German shepherds are smart, strong, hardworking, and loyal dogs.

8

But not all these dogs will complete the tough three-month training. Dogs who don't learn well will become pets for loving families.

◁ *Part of a police dog's training is done on a leash, as seen here.*

Obedience Commands

During training, officers teach their dogs **obedience commands** (oh-BEE-dee-ents kuh-MANDZ). Some obedience commands are "**Heel**" (HEEL), "Stay," and "Come." Commands are taught with words and hand signals. K-9s must learn to obey all their partners' commands, even from far away.

Another part of K-9 training is the **obstacle course** (OB-stuh-kul KORS). The dogs practice **agility** (uh-JIL-uh-tee) skills. They learn to climb ladders, jump over walls, and crawl through small openings. These are skills they might need when chasing criminals.

Police dog training can be tough. But a dog who is right for the job can handle ▷ the harder parts of training.

Criminal Apprehension

Criminal apprehension (KRIH-muh-nul a-pree-HEN-shun) means the capture of criminals, or people who have broken the law. During training, K-9s learn to stop criminals who are trying to run away by jumping on them or by biting their clothing and holding on to them. Police dogs do not try to hurt people, however. A K-9 will stop and hold a **dangerous** (DAYN-jer-us) criminal until his partner takes over.

K-9s are also trained to stop anyone who tries to hurt their partners. This is called **handler protection** (HAND-ler proh-TEK-shun).

Police dogs learn how to hold a criminal without hurting the person.

13

Tracking

Tracking (TRA-king) means following a trail. It is used to find criminals who have escaped or people who are lost. K-9s can use their sensitive noses to follow trails of smells that are on the ground and in the air.

Each person has a different smell, or **scent** (SENT). Our sweat, breath, and old skin cells leave our scent wherever we go. Dogs can tell one person's scent apart from another person's scent. During their tracking training, K-9s learn to track one scent and ignore other scents that might distract them.

Tracking is where a dog's strong sense of smell is put to work. ▷

14

Search Training

Search training is an important part of K-9 training. It's kind of like hide-and-seek. During search training, a trainer hides in the woods. "Find him," an officer commands his K-9. The dog races forward, sniffing trees and bushes. Suddenly he paws at a tree and barks. The dog is saying he's found what he's searching for. This is called **alerting** (uh-LER-ting). Some K-9s alert by sitting still. Others scratch at what they've found. Officers learn to understand their partners' signals. The K-9s practice finding trainers who are hiding in buildings and even in boxes.

◁ *Search training goes on wherever a criminal can hide, including the woods.*

K-9 on the Job

An officer and his K-9 have finished their training. Now they are on patrol. The dog sits in a wire cage in the police car. He looks out the window.

Suddenly the officer stops the car. A man with a knife is trying to hurt someone. The officer opens the cage. "Watch him," he commands. The dog walks toward the man. The man drops his knife and **surrenders** (suh-REN-derz).

People are often afraid of big dogs. Police dogs can **prevent** (pre-VENT) crime and **violence** (VY-oh-lents) just by being nearby.

A police dog can help by guarding the police car while his partner ▷ checks out a crime scene.

A Building Search

A police officer gets a call. A burglar is hiding inside a warehouse. The police need a K-9's help. "This is the police," the officer shouts into the warehouse. "I have a trained dog. Come out or I'll turn him loose!"

Some criminals do what the police say because they are scared of police dogs. But this burglar does not obey. "Find him," the officer commands. He turns his dog loose. The dog tracks the burglar and alerts his partner that he has found the criminal. Then the dog stands guard by the burglar until the officer arrives.

◁ *A building search may be done by both a police dog and his partner.*

Going Home

A busy K-9 like Jesse can spend a whole day searching for a criminal, finding illegal drugs in a warehouse, or finding a stolen wallet. But sooner or later a K-9 and his partner will go home. Jesse and Officer Charles have had a busy day fighting crime, and they're hungry. But before supper they will always play.

Is this frisky dog the same dog who growls at burglars? Is he the same dog who would risk his life to protect his partner? Yes! And tomorrow Jesse will use his skills again to help Officer Charles keep our world safe from crime.

Glossary

agility (uh-JIL-uh-tee) Being able to move around easily.

alerting (uh-LER-ting) Signaling.

criminal apprehension (KRIH-muh-nul a-pree-HEN-shun) To catch or capture a person who has broken the law.

dangerous (DAYN-jer-us) Something that can cause harm.

German shepherd (JER-mun SHEH-perd) A type of large dog with pointed ears.

handler protection (HAND-ler proh-TEK-shun) A K-9's job of making sure his partner is safe.

"Heel" (HEEL) The command for a dog to walk or stand next to its master.

K-9 or **canine** (KAY-nyn) The family of animals that dogs belong to.

obedience commands (oh-BEE-dee-ents kuh-MANDZ) Words or actions that tell you what to do.

obstacle course (OB-stuh-kul KORS) A situation that presents many challenges.

patrol (puh-TROHL) When an officer walks or drives around an area to make sure it stays safe.

prevent (pre-VENT) To keep something from happening.

scent (SENT) The smell of something or someone.

surrender (suh-REN-der) To give up.

tracking (TRA-king) Following a trail.

violence (VY-oh-lents) Rough or harmful action.

Index